MILLENNIAL PHILOSOPHY

THOUGHTS EXPANDED

ADESHINA I. M. LAWAL

MILLENNIAL PHILOSOPHY

THOUGHTS EXPANDED

By

Adeshina I. M. Lawal

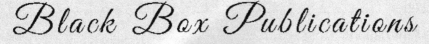

Black Box Publications

The Only Thing Left After The Fire

Millennial Philosophy: Thoughts Expanded. ©

Black Box Live Publications

02-19-2019

Table of Contents

OPEN LETTER

It is with great pleasure and pain that I bring this collection of essays and poems to you. I hope that my words speak to you clarifying the rationality of a Millennial born in Atlanta. This collection follows themes of passion, spirituality, brotherhood and government. I draw on my experiences and raw emotion as the first-generation product of Nigerian descent. These pieces can be read in order, or by selection. I hope you enjoy my tales.

Love's Affirmation

I am worthy of love, just as others are worthy of my love. It is not fair to love others so much, but never to express it. I must not allow my fear of being rejected or being misunderstood to block my expression of love because in doing so I cut off access to feeling one of the most beautiful emotions known to man. Today I will both share and receive love.

MIDNIGHT HIKE

Stop and smell the autumn scent traveling through the midnight air.

I arrest myself to share the moment while take a hike in the middle of the night.

She was tight while I was loose from a quarter bottle of Grey Goose.

To tell the truth we wanted cigars but we didn't wanna take our cars, we took a hike in the middle of the night.

Her conversation had my mind wound up tight whilst her body looked right under autumn moonlight.

White widow's bite left impolite sentiments as we vent to each other.

Our eyes undress each other while confessing our sins for each other.

Our fingertips caress each other as we lock hands.

Under midnight moonlight we stop and tear at each other because we knew from the start we were ripe with sexual passion.

After confession under cool moonlight our hike lit a fire of desire burning ever brighter till the morning light.

THE MENTALITY OF DOMESTIC VIOLENCE

I knew of a mother who was beaten in front of her children because she wished to practice Christianity because the father was a Muslim. If she was seen with a Bible she was beaten and ridiculed. The taunting went on for years until the father had a spiritual epiphany and he himself converted over to Christianity. This kind of abuse is horrific. Even though the man converted to Christianity his abusive tendencies continued on. The mother stayed in the abusive relationship because she felt she had an obligation to keep her family together. She often financially supported the man at times. His abuse was a reflection of his personal fears and failures. He took them out on her to keep control of her time, energy, and resources. She later feels as though the abuse scarred her children as much as it scarred herself. Was the relationship worth the torment and the scars?

Domestic violence on any front is unacceptable. Those who agitate domestic violence- either physically or psychologically- need further state attention be that in a mental institution, incarceration or both. No one is removing the blame from the attacker and placing it on the victim. Rather it is my goal to empower the victim with more knowledge of self; to impart the loving feeling of acceptance and community to an individual who is is treated lesser by an injuring, toxic individual.

Why it that women and men stay in toxic relationships? People stay with partners who do not benefit them in the long run. How many of us have been in a relationship and saw no fruit from the time and resources lost on an unsavory individual? To straggle along a failed relationship is one thing, but to be dragged along in an abusive relationship is another. Why is it that strong women and men surrender themselves and their resources to an individual in exchange for traumatization? Rationally it makes no sense. But in reality, it makes more sense than one spouse paying rent on the 4th, going grocery shopping on the 5th, and one spouse getting beaten by the other on the 6th. Women and men subject themselves to toxic, abusive relationships for a variety of reasons.

From the outside looking in it is easy to wonder how people can stay in such an environment; how easy it would be to escape. But it is not always so easy. This is America. Here - as I'm am sure is so in many cultures- people need their needs met. People have economic and emotional needs that need to be fulfilled. Some people stay with abusive individuals because the relationship gives them a false validation of themselves for whichever reason. Others simmer in an abusive relationship because one partner is economically dependant on the other.

Courage and self-awareness will be critical in overcoming the mental grip the attacker has over the victim. Understand that the attacker in domestic abuse has a personal issue within themselves that they cast on individuals they feel they control; their inadequacies eat at them and boil up in the relationships they enter into.

When attackers get with a strong person, they feel they can manipulate they latch on to them to sustain their ego. Understand that abusive people are parasites. They are weak minded individuals who need to emotionally drain others to sustain their fragile egos. Their abuse will affect the person they are in a relationship with and everyone associated with them. Domestic violence is unfair. If you know anyone going through domestic violence build a relationship with them. Let them know that it is not ok what they are going through. Let them know that it is not the status quo and that there are services available to get them out of that environment and into another. As a society I am glad that we care to support our fellow Americans and their right to live in a community where there is growth and development rather than abuse and neglect.

ANGEL FIRE

The sun was shining when I kissed her.

It never occurred to me that she was an angel in disguise.

My eyes lit up to her radiant body.

In all actuality I was distracted by her psyche and beauty.

I don't take mental sexually lightly.

She might be the one for me but I know that God has kept her out of my

reach so I continued to preach the gospel of love.

I never cage a beautiful beloved dove.

My soul demands her but my body frees love.

I spot her and kiss her forehead.

I shed the coat of world war and we share the robe of love God gave us.

I thrust my body with hers.

Angelic fire consumed our physical structures until they burned away.

She's the one I prayed for, but I can not detour from the charge God has

given me for I must destroy her enemies.

I'm not sure what power she has granted me but I will guard it with my heart

entirely.

Do not weep for me for I have seen true beauty in her mind.

In time I will see my angel again.

A KNIGHT IN BURNT ARMOR

Why does she love me with some much fire?

Her passion derived from her desire for me.

With fury in her eyes she cries out to me.

Weeping she wonders why she loves me.

With her tongue she lashes out at me.

I let out a false smile to let her know that her tumultuous love did not phase me.

Some days she praises me.

I her king and she my queen.

She sees my love as unquestionably authentic.

On other days to her my presence is acidic and sadistic to her every pore.

She would rather be gored by the world's hate than caressed by my ever-loving stroke.

My heart never choked, but nor did my behavior.

Consider me her knight in black armor.

I recognize my Queen's distress and keep it close to my chest.

As she lays on my breast her fears brought to rest.

I attest to slaying her irrational fears with unconditional love. Daily.

Crazily, I stay with her.

Infatuated by her wicked lips I keep my shield ready for our next fiery expression.

PASSION DEFINED

How many times have you heard about an intense crime committed between two lovers? Better still why is it that a mother's words can cut deeper than a stranger's? They say do what you love and you will never work a day in your life. I find love and passion to be of the same origin but serving different purposes. They are both seniors in the hierarchy of emotion. Love and passion have been known to produce either the most beautiful of moments or the most heinous of acts known to man.

If a man is passionate towards the woman that he loves he will express the nature of his desire in an extreme fashion, especially when passion is involved. If a woman is passionate about the career, she has chosen she will divert as much of her time and resources into her endeavor as emotionally possible. Love and passion can create tunnel vision. When someone is engaged in tunnel vision only one objective seems clear- such a nature produces crimes of passion and cute aggression.

In love with another, man has been known to slaughter his brother in an utter blind rage. In his tunnel vision he saw not his brother but rage and its target. He saw blasphemy and betrayal spewing from his brother and his lover. As such he was pushed to slaughter them both. Passion and love are two powerful emotions. Love and passion don't always have to be connected to a romantic notion. Both emotions definitely invoke the idea of romanticism but because these emotions are so robust, they can produce an array of responses from an individual and the collective on an international scale.

From a national level such emotions can provoke a fundraiser for the victims of an earthquake, or allot to the systematic application of eugenics to amplify a perceived master race. Whatever the outcome from a moment of love and passion I guarantee heavy emotional investment. Such emotions have an illogical nature. Common sense can dictate a perfectly reasonable response to a situation while the love and passion duo will more often than not out muscle the most macho of men. Love and passion can destabilize an entire economy lest we forget the lesson learned from Helen of Troy. I do not believe that these two emotions are exact equivalences. Consider the emotion hate.

You can hate something with a passion and seek it's utter destruction, but you couldn't apply the same level of passion to destroy something you love. It will pain you to suffer that which you love. Let's consider the man and his wife again. With intense passion they made love but he kept that same energy when he stabbed her to death when he caught her having sex in his home with his brother. I believe hatred and love are separated by passion and its intensity. There are many reasons to love and to hate; I believe that passion is the intensity level you put into the emotion. The more intense you perceive your passion to be the more erratic your love or hatred will appear. Passion produces mania. Love and hate produce feral artistic expression. Regard passion similar to gasoline whereas love and hate like fire. The more intense you feel passion the hotter and more chaotic love and hatred appear.

I am not as passionate about my hatred for peanuts as I am as erratic about my hatred for snakes- both literally and figuratively. Ultimately it goes to say that passion is fuel for love and hate. Indeed, passion is fodder to the human arsenal of emotion. I find people blessed to have the tool of passion at our dispatch. I do not believe that passion can be contained. Passion can be compared to lava being held back in an erupting volcano. Once the volcano is allowed to express its situation it will do so in a savage manner. The more passionate you are the harder it is to ignore or stifle. I cannot tell you to ignore or express your feelings of passion, but I will ask that you respect the power of passion in your life and others least you restrain an active volcano at your own detriment.

WOMEN IN POLITICS

It is my understanding that the women's delegation will be paramount in this political season. It was the middle to upper class women who gave Trump favor in his election; the #MeToo movement and movements of the sort are falling men left and right. The Republican party will lose Congress to a more independent female constituency. This is not a bad thing. Women are a key component in our society. As such I believe that their voice should be heard.

Their voices have been muffled for a long time in our society. There have been many great female exemplar leaders in the past. Their rationally is no better or worse than that of a man. It is my opinion that their voices be heard equally. Because women have been stifled for so long, they have developed into a more independent counterpart. Their voice will be loud because of the injustices they face in an increasingly less male dominant country.

I feel that men and women should listen to one another. They should come together to mull over the facts. We as a people should know how to have decency and respect one another in our community. There are many men in positions of power that abused their position with their genitals and salaries, but there are many women who have done so as well. Please understand that there are many more men out there who have not done so-men who have quality relationships with their mothers. Men could do a better job with courtesy but so also could ladies. When women go to the election booth they will have an answer for the misogyny they have witnessed. I pray they consider the independent political spectrum.

LOVE'S PATIENCE

How frustrated we get with the ones we love.

We shove our hopes and thoughts down their throats hoping they swallow our passion.

The unnecessary traction creates friction and fire, the perfect contradiction to the passion we desire.

Can you bare to slow down and drown out the fires of this world?

Can we protect our oak tree love as it grows?

We know the mighty oak grows powerful over decades.

Patience aids in it's growth, so also to our love.

Truelove patiently waits through the pressure to create a diamond.

Commissioned at the gem's birth it is little more than Ash.

Love and patience rehash the ash to the perfect diamond I wish for your hand.

I can make no demand as I diligently wait for your patience to grow.

I glow with pride knowing my love's patience approaches my own.

My throne is hers.

CAPTIAN HOOK'S GIRLFRIEND

I love her like no other for my heavy heart flies all a flutter.

She makes me feel like her soldier of love; Sade's passion.

Throughout her body is send the sweetest contractions.

I'm relaxing, knowing my love is forever everlasting.

Adding to our lessons on love we reopened the book to take a look and rewrote the bitch.

She got me shook and hooked in her good book, Captain Hook but I'll never wreck.

We stay up late, talking shit and getting lit on literature chest to neck.

I feel so blessed without her I'd be shipwrecked, perplexed as to my next step.

I need her and she bleeds for me so we see our future in duality, two covers of a good book.

Now take a look at our love, but only for a moment.

Through the amazement take great care not to stop and stare at our love.

My beloved's beauty stands tantamount to looking up when the sun out.

Lookout for Icarus as you stare too closely to our sun.

I pray that this message finds you on angel's wings.

My heart sings for you since we both met.

Emptiness and sorrow filled my soul because a hole was present, better yet a mole was present.

Constantly making mountains from their hills.

Once I broke the mountain and the mole and the departed it was on angel's wings that your message came onto me.

With passion and compassion your lyrics sung to me.

My heart sang back.

We sang harmonious notes of yearning and belonging.

Acceptance matched with curiosity we depart. But My thoughts of you do not.

I long for my angel's next response, rested on her wings once again.

MANIC DEPRESSANT KISSES

I love you I hate you...

Get out of the house but don't leave the room

Doom and gloom in your eye

You push me away while drawing me closer

Our love is like an emotional rollercoaster

Our bodies twisted together like a pretzel

Intertwined in sensual pleasure and pain

Slain by your stressors I'd kill for you

I witness the duality of your personality

Two sides of the same coin

Your value never diminished by your pain

Your fractures make you so beautiful

For the nature of our bond is bountiful.

SONGS OF LOVE

If our relationship were a song what what would it sound like?

Would it be reminiscent of a slow motion love song from the 70's?

Heavenly, So smooth and soulful.

Would it call back to the roaring 20's?

Bent knee big band love making symphony.

Could our love be the soulful erratic strummings of a 90's punk rock band?

We stand it's us against the world, no it's fuck the world for our love.

I would hope that our love punches with the power of a trap-tastic hip hop track from 2001, with all due respect to those concerned.

Could our love sound like a new song?

Angelic harmonies that only you and I can render, but we forgot the notes.

We play sheet music everyday to keep the notes of our Harmony in motion.

PORTRAIT OF VENUS

If I could paint a picture perfect portrait of Venus...Her body would remind me of the river Nile powerful and mighty, yet gentle enough to sustain life.

Her eyes would sing the notes of passion humming ever so sweetly; they speak so eloquently, hitting every key note of melody.

That her knowledge be like the first pick of summer strawberries, ever so sweet and succulent to the lips.

Let her passion burn like a wildfire for I am a cancer. Whenever and wherever water and fire come together steam always resides.

May her thighs remind me of the thickest chocolate, smooth and viscus ooh so mighty in essence.

Hope that our connection points to the sun in relation to the moon. They gravitate to one one another in such a way as only celestial bodies can.

Pray that her spirit remind me of the dove, pure and free. As clean and fresh as winter snow, cuffed only to The good Lord and myself... Is this too much to ask for?

BLACK VIRGIL

Greetings to you all.

I come to you in a time of extraordinary division.

I envision the extinction of our way of life if we allow strife and hatred to control our minds.

Our wives and children pay the price if we allow a false Antichrist to separate that which cannot be broken.

I am open to close the wounds and to ice the bruises our Constitution accrued.

With our alluding minds as buffers we can stand tougher than American steel.

We must stand still and chill the hate between our brothers.

Mother Earth birthed us all but it is up to us to trust one another least we lose ourselves and destroy each other.

The false Antichrist uses fear and ignorance to prevent solidarity while promoting anarchy.

The enemy of hatred is love; love's heavenly weaponry is peace and accountability.

Add in chivalry and rationally and we can all snap back to reality.

Sadly it takes pain and suffering to open the soul.

Truth be told love and understanding separate segregation from our congregation.

Dedication to brotherly love serves as amplification to our federation.

My patience for honest communication stands equivalent to the desperation of a starving man with a master plan can you overstand?

HATE

When I think of hate I think of fear. Fear is an emotion much like hate. It is as though they feed each other. We fear what we don't understand and we hate it for that, I guess. I'm afraid of snakes- they give me a super cold feeling in the pit of my stomach. This being said when I see them, I wish to kill them because I hate them. Like I said hate and fear are natural emotions; they are witnessed at scale. I do not believe that they are always related. I do not fear nor hate a racist because I understand them. I see them as an opportunity for engagement- engagement is also at scale. Perhaps I should learn to understand snakes better, but that may take more time and self-control.

PROBLEMS

Is it in human nature to create problems where none exist? We as a people, in order to maintain an imperfect union reject coming together. Such behavior creates problems for other people to fix or pay the bill for. I don't believe that this issue is specific to any particular place or ethnicity; I do believe it is not confined to any set socio economic grouping. Sometimes people create issues on purpose. Other times problems are created because of choices made leading up to problems on problems.

Problems can even arise by fortune of pure chance. If you believe in fate you can see how problems can arise for no other reason than you being tested by God. It wasn't until I was fired from my job and becoming unable to acquire conventional stress relief that I began to write. Time has passed and I have since gotten other jobs. I continue to write because I see the value in it; I found its value within a problem.

For whatever reason problems exist in our lives to make you stronger. Problems both expose the true nature and character of an individual. In retrospect problems serve as an excellent source of knowledge applicable to future successes. Whenever faced with a problem remember that your perception and mentality will dictate how you approach the problem. Problems will also shed light on people and materials in your environment that you can use towards your success.

Is it possible to ignore ignorance?

Indeed ignorance blasts from it's producer stronger than the loudest

Trump supporter.

Thorn in my side sworn to fall even the most powerful Spartan.

But can I overcome ignorance?

Absolutely.

Ignorance hardens its opposite suitor.

I harvest patience knowing that I must temper my temper.

Surely the louder I confronted ignorance the harder it punched back.

Ignorance beat my ass a few times.

Had me swear that ignorance was a flame I was butter.

I utter to God for help but...

God left me outside on a hot summer afternoon to lick my own wounds.

Ignorance left many scars on me.

I wasn't liquified but the ignorance was still flaming hot.

I discovered that I was steel, untempered steel.

Ignorance was a fire meant to harden me.

Ignorance prepares me for the battles up ahead.

Had I not done such battle with ignorance her weak flame would burn me.

Now with the fruits of battle I can reach into the gut of ignorance and

retrieve my comrades unharmed.

WHO SHOT CHIVALRY?

When a man opens the door for a lady what would you expect?

On the one hand it is an extension of mannerisms risen from home training.

Remaining seated as a lady joins or leaves a table is fabled to be bad taste.

Faced with journeying down a street with a lady have the man closer to the road, a lady is never to walk the street.

He brought roses to her mother, and smoked cigarettes with her father.

All fuel for the fodder; She shot chivalry.

Indiscriminately slaughtered in her lust for ignorance.

They called him thirsty as they lusted for dope dick and a bill.

Or they sold their flower to the highest bidder forgetting that bidders frequent auctions.

Chivalry was murdered- the gentleman has been falsely outranked by the thug.

Hoodlums amount to little, but a gentleman...

A gentleman can blossom into a syndicate.

A gentleman will calculate further than arithmetic.

They move like calculus.

They operate on trust.

They abide by the code.

The code is simple.

All women are reminiscent of your mother clustered with your sister.

They are a collective, show respect- men, submit to your lady in they hope they submit to you.

Chivalry rested with trust. Trust was kidnapped and lost her partner.

MOVING DAY

A friend of mine called me and said her mom was moving. She asked me if I could help. As fortune had it I had a couple of items left over from my last move that needed to be brought to my new spot. I asked if she could help me transport my items, and I would help her mom move her house the next day. She came by that night and helped me pick up the items. The next morning I rose early, we joined forces and proceeded to her mom's house.

Her mom had boxes on boxes. Heavy appliances, chairs, and tables were a foot. The rooms had been compartmentalized and compressed so we were ready to get the items on the truck in an organized fashion. It was myself and two other guys in addition to the mother and daughter. I find the whole process of people moving very interesting: how people pack, how they load, where they live, and where they are going. I may even consider what kind of packing materials are on hand and how well those materials are being put to use. Organization plays a huge factor as well. Moving day is a main event.

I feel as though how we move is not as important as why we move. Sometimes we move to expand the amount of space necessary to fit our current position. Other times we move to have a reduction in unnecessary space. We may move to better suit our relationship status, for better or worse. If you move to flee a past situation you may leave a few or all of your possessions; consider this a rebirth. If you plot out a move because your taking on a bigger economic role consider the move a bold investment. If you are moving to further kindle a romantic flame consider it a leap of faith.

All in all moving day is a step into the unknown. You leave a familiar location for one that will be different in many ways; there will always be familiar features and new neighbors. Pack all your past experiences into boxes and move them to a new location. Learn and build from those experiences in a new location to see if you can better pilot the future of new experiences.

I finished up helping my friend's mom move, but I ended up being an hour late to work. Even though my day was thrown off I still had an aire of satisfaction and accomplishment for helping my friend's mom move while acquiring the last of the items left at my last dwelling. When you move, you may have to throw a lot of items away. You may forget a few items at the spot you are leaving. Indeed, you may need to buy some items for the new spot. We strive to build satisfaction for ourselves in our places of rest. We keep a collection of the past and future future hopes in boxes we call our home. Just remember the final box the body goes in. On that moving day will your soul be satisfied?

With love and power I greet you.

My thoughts after we meet still persistent and insistent on your well-being.

I love you.

Seeing you gives me hope.

My energy acts as a rope as I reel you in.

Genuine is my love for you, a stranger in my mind.

I find the special sauce within you and demand that it boils.

My energy makes you simmers.

The humdrum nature of your everyday life shaken to awaken your spices.

Your vices brought to light.

Your first response may be frightening rejection of my manhood.

I welcome the unknown in you.

Truth be told I am bold enough to question my existence.

My eyes intense drawing you to my order.

Every step I take like a soldier.

A sniper's shot- lethal and intended.

You know I'd kill for you, but you are unsure of my target, those who are not of the like.

Those whose soul and heart have gone completely dark.

They too may join me, but they must submit to enlightenment.

My soul channels the beautifications of wisdom and love.

My presence asserts my continence for anyone in thought's range.

Captivating.

POWER SPREAD

I'm running three steps forward yet taking two steps back, every moment

I'm pushing limits, ttg on attack.

I'm ready to relax but my persistence is on max. I've hit success like a drug

and I need that shit back.

Every failure a catalyst and every partnership adrenaline.

I'm a true southern gentleman, tell a friend.

With a chip on my shoulder, that often feels like a boulder I soldier my my

burden.

Im dark and strong like straight Folgers my patience bled out; my views on

the world become colder and bolder.

There's no cut in my dedication my thoughts are pure melanin.

Standing ten toes tall watch my power spread.

PRECISION

Would a surgeon use a jackhammer to remove a heart, or would he use a scalpel as well as an assortment of other tools to accomplish the job? When looking for precision it is important to use the right tool do the job. Oftentimes we get stuck in quicksand wrestling with the wrong tool to towards success. Consider the surgeon and the jackhammer. He may have proper coordination, dexterity, and even a scalpel at his disposal. If he is hell bent on using the jackhammer he will kill every patient he sees, but if he becomes aware of using a scalpel alongside the rest of a surgical arsenal his success rate will skyrocket. The more intuition one has the more precise he shall be. Life is like this: always look to the best tool when doing a job. Finding that tool may require looking into oneself, observing others in action, or reading a book.

SCARS OF THE FATHER

Fathers often try to mold their sons in a better image of themselves.

They look through the shelves of their past inadequacies and cut incisions into their son's personality.

These incisions can lead to fatalities.

Those fathers realize that their failures could have been avoided had they been better prepared for the danger.

In anger they make incisions on their sons. Sometimes with the precision of a surgeon, but often with the passion of an overzealous hunter.

Some fathers are not even present.

In a moment of ignorant clarity they flee the scene for whatever weakness they assume is relevant.

The scars of abandonment appear all the more infected.

The maim from abandonment allows a deep dose of personality poisoning to set in.

Resentment joins in and and calls for aggression to accompany the infected affliction.

Questions of self identity and quality go unanswered until the wrong time.

Rewind to the child's birth.

Remember that this boy did not request this Earth; your activities did.

You expressed manhood to produce him.

Take your kin and consider your code.

Expose the scars your father left, with a scalpel cut correct.

As is human nature mistakes will be made.

Take shade in understanding the causal clients of time and knowledge.

Surgeons do not rush a critical operation.

With clear-cut calculation they make their marks.

They take care not introduce toxins into their environment.

Surgeons remove the bad and increase the good; they do so with their hands, eyes, nose, and mind.

They do not take a blind eye to their mistakes and their ignorance.

Fathers should emulate surgeons and not demolition men when considering the scars a father will render.

JADED HATRED

Your jaded hatred has you spitting obscenities from your lips in front of the children.

Your abomination towards your cousin stuffs your lungs and blood with boiling poison compelling you to infect others.

You seek to pass judgement against your brother only on his color while you think you will never stand trial for murder.

Society has been impregnated with jaded hatred and she is almost ready to give birth to the accursed spawn of his overzealous seed.

See the germ of jaded hatred on a multicultural scale- witness the many levels of hell.

Jaded hatred produces widespread poverty for the many, but it must occur on an individual level in order to survive thriving off individual lies.

Snuff out the enemy of peace and bring him forward to explain his backward thought process latched to jaded hatred.

When circulated it oozes from their eyes as if they were gripped by an anaconda controlled by the Devil.

It takes generations to achieve jaded hatred as it must be birthed by a lie and spread over time with obscenities and acts of intolerant nonsense.

Peace must be absent in order for hatred to become jaded, but when peace is achieved on an individual level jaded hatred can be bled out.

Never doubt the power of peace and love for together they are the anti venom to jaded hatred.

Their anti venom works with such determinism that they are persistent enough to run counterter-contamination against jaded hatred. This cure must occur on an individual level on a biracial scale bringing part to whole rendering jaded hatred starving.

KILLING ANGELS

You fear what you do not understand, you choose to destroy angels.

You suffer in your private place, so you make others suffer publicly for your pain.

In bloodstained savagery you feel no emotion, therefore causing pain on others releases your inner pain bottled up, long overdue.

These tormentors can be saved, but but love, hope, and knowledge must be sought.

In thought an angel can appear on Earth and be rejected for his difference.

Intense scrutiny will be upon him.

On top of that tormentors will swarm him.

Mainly because he is misunderstood.

The tormentor who destroyed what he ununderstood can still serve good.

But he must be like the seed the sewer threw on good land.

On second hand some tormentors attack those who remind them of their inner pain.

They remain on the hunt to injure others, catharsis to their hurting.

Once love and reality make incisions on his heart he's desire to do malice bleeds out.

To the one who enjoys bloodshed all is not lost.

God can emboss thoughts of love and chivalry on anybody.

Through him a new hobby will be given.

Like Saul when became Paul God has power over all.
We must answer the phone when the Supreme Being calls, lest we fall
into the old habit of killing Angels hope and all.

COMPOSITE BETRAYAL

Shot in the back by composite bow my brother knows me well.

I can always smell my enemy's burning fuse combined with gunpowder presented for my demise.

My two eyes never surprised by the lethality that my enemy possesses.

Yes, I know that my enemy confesses poisonous arrows to my manhood regularly but an assassination attempt on my character that takes my breath away.

Yeah, The constriction I now endure in my chest caused by my delayed reaction

Contractions in my heart giving me new lessons in understanding aggression by hands blood related

Blood is thicker than water but so is oil

I toil with trust in comrades

Gunshots From an enemy are more easily detected and deflected than a brother's silent arrow drawn back on composite bow.

I'm not white, but I'm not black.

I'm not Nigerian but I'm not American.

I'm not Republican, but I'm definitely not a Democrat.

I'm an American African and I straddle the fence.

I'm constantly in defense of who I am perceived to be.

Truthfully I fully understand Slim Shady's dilemma.

I am what you say I'm not and am.

I am an independent.

Authenticated by antiquated home training.

My parents remind me I wasn't American, and my peers reminded me I wasn't Nigerian...

How Shakespearean of a conflict.

I've seen every side of Atlanta yet Santa cannot deliver pure ebonics to my dialect.

Folks check my negro resume and revoke my black card.

I'm barred by my skin color and intellect from surviving long enough in the American economy.

I simply do not fit the pure American mold.

I am too bold to be sold into economic slavery.

I am too proud to stand by lazily and consume government cheese.

I refuse to slide by by knees to the DFCS office after acquiring a $140k degree.

When I was in college and working they couldn't supplement me.

Had I dropped out of school they would have saved me.

Honestly my Nigerian American pride stays with me.

I was trained to stand, walk, and talk like a man.

I was raised to speak with authority.

Now they try to condition me so speak sweetly.

Discreetly they wish to castrate the God in me.

I refuse.

I endure the attacks on my character knowing I have been blessed with alabaster oil over my entire body.

I admire Jesus Christ who gave his body for international saving grace.

I embrace the Prophet Muhammad who went into isolation and meditation only to return with the word of God.

I too carry a holy message and have been rejected by the very people who murdered Jesus.

Atlanta is my Acropolis and I its Prodigy.

I refuse to surrender becoming a pretender against what I am.

I forever am the Nigerian American Spartan with a plan connected to Ever loving hope.

I stand rock hard as a man should although through other people's eyes I appear Shattered like a kaleidoscope.

I elope all sides of my heritage and stand humbled by my authentic authority.

My story is only beginning.

Peace, love, and respect; by any means necessary.

It's not that I'm antisocial.

I'm not postal but I can be considered unstable.

I am not able to follow the other sheep to their stable.

I am Abel surrounded by a flock of Kanes.

Who can connote the origin of man's anger and jealousy?

Technically I separate from Kane's followers and I search for true reality.

Not the version on TV which is scripted, twisted and uplifted, but the one where the meek inherit the Earth.

Kane's flock worships jealousy, ignorance and violence.

It makes sense why I reject and am rejected.

How powerful are the meek?

They are unable to speak loud enough to be heard over Kane's flock's belting.

They too stand separate, segregated from good fortune.

Is it fair to blame capitalism for the acceptance of Kane's flock?

Abel's offering was favored over Kane and he died for it.

Or is human nature to blame, and capitalism only a vehicle?

Biblically jealousy, envy, and greed have been the seeds necessary to feed Kane's flock.

These seeds also bloom capitalism and her fruits.

I do not seek to stockpile my fruit, but to enjoy them with the meek.

Kane's flock is obsolete and should not be allowed to speak.

CAST OFF HERITAGE

In the antebellum period of America the southern slaves would wear what they called cast off clothing. The term was given to the clothing because the cloths did not fully robe you, but they could easily be taken off for work or beating purposes. That manner of clothing has expired but I wonder if the phrase could be reengineered. Consider hatred heritage. Much like cast off clothing hatred heritage can sometimes be seen as a bondage. Hatred can be translated through heritage.

If you put a baby from a member of the Ku Klux Klan with a baby from a member of the Black Panther Party the two would almost certainly love each other. Give them 10 years of socialization and that could easily change. I am not the enemy to heritage, but the defender of diversity. What we teach the youth most definitely matters. Many features of heritage are wonderful. I can not help but feel that many features of heritage are enslaving our population.

We now live in a world where cultural information is readily available; likewise the people from which the culture derives from are easily accessible. As an adult you must reflect upon the heritage you were given. Assess the knowledge you have been given and weigh it against the wisdom available in the world. By doing this you may see the benefits your culture provides, or you may realize the errors of antiquated philosophies and include new knowledge to pass on to future generations that will better equip them as they navigate an international community.

PEACE CONSIDERED

One might ask how peace can be described. When I first considered peace, I saw the emotion as an energy signature much like passion. Peace is a state of mind stemming from an individual which ripple through whichever environment the individual finds themself in. Can peace be found in a chaotic environment; likewise can chaos be included into a peaceful environment undetected? I would venture to say that the former is more possible than the latter, but with conditions attached. To find peace in chaos is to find absolute serenity within the individual who exudes said peace while in the eye of the storm.

The individual knows something so prevalent about their situation that their knowledge allows them to maintain peace. Interestingly enough the introduction of chaos into serenity should be detected almost immediately. To be at peace doesn't necessarily mean that all thing are positive, and to carry chaos doesn't mean the possession of evil -this is why the concept of organized chaos carries such weight. An individual who is at peace within their person controls their own environment, even if their environment carries chaotic signatures. They are even able to create peacefully in such an environment.

Sometimes chaos is necessary to bring about peace and personal growth. On a larger scale such is the nature of revolution. Society can be at peace with negative notions- having fallen asleep to better options. The introduction of chaos jarrs society to respond to pressure, thus creating change. Consider the American Women's Suffrage campaign or President Theodore Roosevelt and his Trust-Busting operation. These operations went against the status quo but for the betterment of society.

The collective has been at peace with the subjugation of individuals within society- I am certain that some women accepted the notion that it was ok for their husbands to beat them whenever they saw fit. Look into the phrase "Rule of Thumb" for inspiration. Peace is absolutely necessary for positive human existence. No soul can handle extreme scrutiny and duress for a long period of time without peace to dilute the pressure.

Likewise human beings need chaos to jar them from unquestioned existence. People grow when they are presented with chaotic moments, either for good or bad depending on the individual. There is nothing wrong with living in a peaceful environment. It is important to live in peace, but not at the expense of someone else's chaos- least the one in chaos violates your peace and you consider them a savage.

BLACK ON BLACK

I remember the phrase "packing like Mexicans". One would see two or three Hispanic families living together under the same roof. They ate the necessities and dressed basically. Truly they sacrificed and suffered; indeed they relied on God's power and personal sacrifice. We can not assume what happened behind closed doors, but from the outside looking in they seemed to be like the parable of the ant and the grasshopper. The ant like the Hispanic family structure and the grasshopper like the black family structure. Many a time my biggest obstacles have a skin tones like mine, or they are of the fairer variety.

Why is it that we separate from each other on so many levels? I feel as though we as a people disrespect the hustle but praise money. All praise is the Lord's. When the Lord chooses to bless the hustle and faithfulness of one of our own the crabs show their faces. Why does he have that? I remember when he wasn't shit. His girl a hoe. Lets rob him. I could go on, but I digress. Success for a group is like climbing a ladder. If you swat at the person above yourself you risk them falling on your head; if you kick at the person below you they may fall on the one who is after them while grasping at your heel to save themselves. Until black folk start encouraging and considering others of the like we are destined to take the hard path to the top. We will be far less likely to turn back and pay it forward.

ON DIVERSITY AND DIVISION

We separate from each other on so many levels, often times to the detriment of society. We cling to archaic notions of ethnic division while forcefully ignoring the common good of a multicultural society. Society looks to place individuals into groupings and attach biases to them. Society rejects the idea that people operate on individual levels while being products of their own environment. Knowing that people are social animals we often group together ultimately forming nation states and international coalitions.

America is composed of many different ethnic groups abiding under the Constitution and its delegates. It is not my desire to consider the legitimacy of the government, but to contemplate the inclusion and division occuring on American soil. Is it ok to be pro-white? Is it ok to be pro-black? Is it ok to be pro-hispanic or pro-asian? I would throw in my lot with yes, so long as your rights end where mine begin.

To agitate inclusion, one must have a desire to become learned. This is not to say that you have to be worldly in order to appreciate diversity. You must only become comfortable with socializing with people who have different dispositions and views from your own. It is ok to identity with whichever group you wish so long as everyone has equal access to life, liberty, and the pursuit of happiness. We must consider what is best for generations to come like our infrastructure.

Diversity can be considered as a group of individuals stemming from different backgrounds who come together for a purpose. This doesn't mean an absolute fusion to the group while stripping identity of self. Diversity is not a melting pot but a mosaic of individual jewels glued together. Our current American model was frozen together with water and is being tested with fire. It is never too late to use Georgia red clay to reset the jewels of our society. This clay can be fired and glossed to make a new American work of art.

One might ask what can be divided from society in a positive manner. I wager hateful and intolerant individuals be cast out from society until they reckon the error of their disposition. To spread hate while promoting violence is criminal. To teach knowledge of self identity and culture is enlightenment. Recognize your identity and be proud of your history, but don't violate a different group as you express your self-worth. If you have to reduce a different group to increase the prominence of your own perhaps the group you have selected isn't as pungent as it seemed at first glance.

I need not put another person down because I am confident in my own right. Likewise I group myself with others who carry the same aire as myself, but come from different backgrounds. By doing this I am constantly learning different things while expressing myself. Diversity is often miscredited with loss of self. I believe that diversity helps in finding oneself. By being exposed to different ways of life you can better find what works best for you on an individual level.

AWARENESS

There are lost opportunities at hand if you do not take knowledge of self as well as discernment for other people to heart. "If you know the enemy and know yourself, you need not fear the result of a hundred battles. If you know yourself but not the enemy, for every victory gained you will also suffer defeat. If you know neither the enemy nor yourself, you will succumb in every battle." These are the words of Chinese Philosopher Sun Tzu. If you know how you will respond to a given situation you typically know how the situation will turn out, but you don't know your adversary's response—therefore you leave room for collateral damage. If you don't know yourself how could you know your enemy? If you do not know your enemy how could you be aware of what risks you assume If you choose to engage?

The term "enemy" should be taken loosely here because there are other types of people in the world. Some people take the form of business partners or friends; if you understand them and yourself you can draw from their strength while strengthening their weaknesses. Some folks appear as similar like minded contemporaries, but are in actuality sheep in wolf's clothing; by discerning their features you can play chess with them to achieve your goals. Know yourself and your counterpart, and in 1,000 interactions you will not be in peril.

COMMON SENSE

Voltaire says that common sense is not so common, but I disagree. It is common sense that elected President Cheeto. It was with common sense that slaves were used to increase the Confederate flag. Common sense murders black men. Common sense dictates grabbing women by the pussy. Common sense praises cut throat capitalism over good will society. Common sense is gauged by popular culture. That which is under common understanding is acceptable by society. Not all features of common sense are ridiculous. It is common sense to eat. Common sense demands taking care of our youth. Common sense dictates gaining knowledge about our environment. Common sense praises taking care of our community. Common sense is guided by time and popular culture. This means that people can control common sense for the betterment or detriment of society and its government.

LEADERSHIP AND A BARBEQUE

Teamwork can be considered as the joint effort of a group of people in order to achieve a collective goal as efficiently and effortlessly as possible. Each individual will have a purpose- sometimes their purpose may overlap with another individual. By utilizing the resources, they have available they are able to achieve said goals. Teamwork requires communication as an integral part of reaching shared objectives. This being said it is imperative that both speaking, listening and respect be a part of the communication thread.

Furthermore, it is quintessential that leadership be present. Leadership adds the resource of informed direction. Leadership draws the resources available together to culminate the vision of shared success. Being a leader can take many forms, and it is something anyone can do. Leaders do not always have to be key decision makers. So long as the doors of communication are open decision makers and other leaders can join their talents together to effectively culminate the dream of success. There will be times of disagreement. Indeed, conflicts will arise. In such cases wise leadership can assess the situation and come up with resolutions to the issue that are beneficial to both parties as well as satisfy the major objective at hand.

Let us consider throwing a barbeque from two different angles. In scenario one I throw the barbeque myself. I wake up in the morning and begin my preparation. I go to the store and grab my produce, protein, carbs;

I will need bell peppers, onions, tomatoes, chicken, beef, cheese, pasta, beans, spices, and sauces. I will need an assortment of aluminum containers, flammable liquids and charcoal. I will need tablecloths as well as tables and chairs fit for outside. Next, I will need to prepare all side dishes and have them chilled for future use later on in the day. I will answer all phone calls and send out all invites for the barbeque. I will then send the eating area and greet all my guests while operating the grill and keeping the dishes clean. I will play with children and entertain my guest... At what point will I eat, use the restroom, and make new connections? Let us look at the same scenario from a different angle.

In scenario two I decide to throw a barbeque utilizing a collective. I call a couple of my comrades to pitch them of my idea. Several feel as though this is a splendid idea. I tell one friend to produce two sides; I tell another friend to produce two more sides. I tell another friend to acquire three types of chips and tell two friends to acquire salsa. I tell another friend to grab two thirty packs of beer. I tell another friend to collect a bottle of liquor and some wine. I go to the store and pick up my meat, a case of beer and wine, propane, charcoal, and table cloths. I ask my neighbor if we could borrow his lawn table and a few lawn chairs as well. The morning of the barbeque I organize. I make phone calls to the barbeque squad to touch bases with their respective objectives. I discover that one side piece bringer will not be able to arrive, but their sides are available for pickup. I am able to send another individual from the guest list to acquire those sides as well as an additional case of beer. I begin the grill. I have time to enjoy my beer and the company of my guests while producing beautiful meat.

Which scenario sounds more enjoyable? A mad man would pick option one over option two. Option two utilizes all the resources available. By communicating the vision of a summertime barbeque to a few friends I am able to to produce a fantastic time for my crew and myself. Teamwork made it possible. Leadership is an inextricable component to teamwork. Without leadership great opportunities can be lost due to lack of direction.

Stressful occurrences can be reduced through utilizing effective teamwork and quality leadership. What emotions can be related to leadership? I would say love, trust, consideration, peace, kindness, perseverance, happiness, and curiosity definitely plug into teamwork. The best leaders know how to follow. To add additional support where necessary. Great leaders are able to have a robust vision and a fine scope to assess whether their vision is gaining traction or not. They have the ability to spread compassion over their whole team. Great leaders can take different individuals and produce magnificent results that add value to the individuals taking part in the situation and the team at large.

Good morning millennials.

Hope all is well knowing damn well a quarter of y'all need bail from jail.

Rent pushing up good luck, I know half of y'all false upscale while three quarters of y'all looking up from hell.

Hormones in food have you swole like Clydesdales but your parents fridge is locked down without bail.

Widespread culture is dead.

Our generation so fed up wanting to buck our student loans cause the government fucked up.

How do you charge $100k large to a brother with no job and cast him to society?

Highway robbery, it's not fair to see society eat while our group cooks the food and they elude that our work ethic is crude- without us you're screwed.

We appear like economic immigrants.

We are the generation of new bootstraps white and black pushing back in random tandem.

Our whole fucking anthem is based on abandoning lessons instilled in us through Americanization.

Imagine a $700 check with the rent marked at $650 and the whip $250.

It's impossible arithmetic and simply a product of our millennial gap.

Please understand student loans are not getting paid back.

Relax paps we got your back with our faces in screens we a attack back in due time.

We will control the supply line, but just hope Russia and China stay on our timeline- we continue to grind out towards succession.

Corporations are the government, but I wonder what they charge for rent. I consent to their law if they pick up the charge I owe to the false government.

They take money from my check for shit I'll never see.

But their salary is guaranteed while they suck us dry; bled out from the neck.

They steal our money and complain about smoking trees.

I'd rather pay Mickey D's $100 Gs to retire me after twenty straight years of salary

Could I build a house just for me and my family?

In reality I have no problem with sharing creativity and our connectivity but we need more love and solidarity to strengthen our economy.

Millennials understand that our nation has been bought but don't be distraught because we stand 10 toes tall.

Though we fall we will soar like the mighty eagle.

We are regal in our own light and are prepared to fight until morning light. Take sight.

Celebratory Family Members

They come around in season expecting gifts.

They make unreasonable demands planned out before hand.

They are celebratory family members.

Pretenders who keep both a hand and an eye out.

They gossip and backbite despite the plight they face in their own lives.

Filled with spite they come to celebrate.

They set the date on their calendar.

All asunder the blasphemer reminisces about the last topic of the last celebration.

It was you.

In lieu of enjoying good company they ask you questions about your current situation.

Anticipation grips them as they want for your pain.

They remain attentive until the pain never arrives.

They thrive in your self pity but you were ready.

You came to feast with family.

Silently you enjoy your meal, but make merriment with family ties thicker than water.

Their love administrator to your presence.

Some family comments take the form of verbal manslaughter.

Kin bloodshed adding fuel and fodder.

Don't bother with petty family members, but feed your soul.

This boldness will starve the soul of petty members forcing them to

celebrate their own misery.

Interestingly they are celebratory family members.

ANUBIS' SCALES

How heavy is your heart?

I knew it from the start that I couldn't take part in the shit that you do.

Anubis' scales will prevail and send your ass straight to hell after

consensus.

The tale of your life fills your heart good or bad, happy or sad.

Ironclad scales weigh your heart against a feather better hope you

enjoyed your life and shared love.

Love lightens the soul and the heart while hate crushes the body with the

pressure of a metric ton.

After death what's left of your heart will be put to test.

Only those who blessed others with love and lightened their hearts may

pass by the stress test against the weight of a feather.

Better now then never lighten your heart by releasing your love's passion.

Only God and his partners may judge because they hold no grudge.

All that's left is pure calculation lacking anticipation for life's end.

Depending on a scale, a feather, and a heart Justice and Love will stand

as counterweights to your fucking fate.

AMERICAN PHILOSOPHY'S CHILDREN

The house negro was disrupted when the field negro learned how to read. Indeed, the house negro had sold themselves to cutthroat capitalism, and regularly attended lynching. That last name- Lynch- still lives on today. So also does that mentality and its children. The community of American Philosophy have had many children. Racism and colorism are but two of them. Innovation and charity are two more. for some odd reason I find that many systemic advancements have been made possible off of the backs of lower socio-economic ranking individuals.

That back has been colored every shade in mankind's likeness, yet they are not treated equally- even among themselves. Ignorance and arrogance are two more children of American philosophy and they need to be put in check. These children committed incest and birthed Donald Trump. In his last visit to the United Nations he was ridiculed by his peers for his boastful erroneous comments. There is nothing wrong with American philosophy's child Pride, but if she chooses not to listen she falls in line with arrogance and foolishness.

You will find that there are many similarities in American philosophy and other national families; their family tree is just structured differently. Is it possible to restructure a cultural family tree? Can members become deceased? Can members marry members of other cultures and produce new thought identities? Can long lost members gain proper recognition?

Can members reflect on their own nature and gain a more clear understanding of themselves, their abilities, and their children? I leave these questions with you.

ELECTING PEERS

If elected officials were paid the median wage of the area they serve while living in a home payable by minimum wage would they still serve? Clearly people do not mind serving their constituents. Firemen, teachers, police officers, and librarians do so on a regular basis. Interestingly enough I have noticed the average wage of state elected officials to be decent for the most part- although there will always be occurrences where public officials fall to corruption. Are there people left in the world who cannot be bought? It seems as though the further elected officials are from their appointers the more likely they will be ravaged by objects unfitting for a proper statesmen.

Are there people out there who cannot be impregnated by scandalous politics? I consider myself to be a George Washington figure. If I were handed all the power in the world, I would hand it back to the people in the hopes that an informed constituency will forever select the best choice. I would accept the standard fare for operation and gain my satisfaction from knowing that I have strengthened my community and my country. I take notes from Ben Frank- arguably one of the most influential Americans on record. I would love life, creativity, and commerce. I would move like Frederick Douglass. I realize the call to action in my life not to accept the status quo, common sense perception of good law. Abraham Lincoln says that we should obey the law- even if it is not good- until popular opinion says otherwise. I cannot accept this.

All too often great leaders parrot taking initiative. Taking initiative demands seeing an issue and taking action on that issue to rectify the situation. I want my determination to be like Colin Rand Kaepernick. He stood ten toes tall in the face of adversity on both sides- from myself as well initially. At first, I questioned his delivery. I considered keeping politics and economics separate. In retrospect I now see the impact that Martin Luther King spoke about. Truly John Lewis adhered to MLK's philosophy since we could not have the man himself.

Carry on Kaepernick. Your boldness is on mankind's record. He spoke not of money but stood for an issue. He made it as large as it could be while he was mocked every step of the way. Take courage from him, even if you don't agree with his philosophy. I take courage from Donald Trump in his use of decisive action. He is not afraid to make a decision or statement and stand by his guns. I take no other ethical notes from the man, and I stand in question of his business tactics. I believe that he is unfit for his position, and that he too has been impregnated by the very swamp that eats him alive now.

Need a ride to work, better call an Uber.

They screw you to insure they take no losses.

The process of being in Atlanta will eat you alive.

It is possible to thrive but you must have tough skin.

Your kin will suffer you, but just enough to keep themselves higher than you.

Your employers will try to fire you when they see you rising, despising seeing a young falcon rising.

Surprising enough that they would rather see you bust that confirm your hustle and worth.

Every paycheck you receive a nail in your coffin; every promotion bringing you closer to your hurst.

But the music is dope though, and the food will make your soul glow.

The struggle will make your heart grow, and you might start rocking fresh ass Polos.

We got people from all over the world, and they brought their driving habits too.

Traffic on 75-85 make you take 285 dude.

If you leave the house 5 minutes late you're screwed.

If you make it in Atlanta you've paid your dues.

You can cruise up and down Moreland like you have nothing to lose.

Catch yourself slipping before someone steals your shoes.

Welcome to Atlanta, birthplace of Freaknik.

Our analytic calculated by heat and passion.

Afro-Rational brought conscious in our cultural melting pot.

Leave a thought and gain Love.

Welcome to Atlanta, the city I belove.

COLORISM EXPLAINED

My girlfriend says " my cousin said I should preserve my skin complexion, and that I would receive preferential treatment if I did so." It was the craziest notion I had heard in a while. She also referred to the difference in treatment one gets if they are "High Yellow". She was in fact shedding light on the question of colorism, but I had not known the theory by this name. I had a conversation with someone else who said that light skinned people had it better than dark skinned people. That light skinned people were given preferential treatment because of their tone. My girlfriend said she was told things like this by her family and close friends, and with straight faces.

Google defines Colorism as discrimination based on skin color, also known as colorism or shadeism, is a form of prejudice or discrimination in which people are treated differently based on the social meanings attached to skin color. It is the categorization of black folks amongst ourselves in order to further separate the black community. I find it interesting how colorism exists in the white community, but not to the weaponized extent that it is in the black community. In the white community it has been deemed socially acceptable to tan frequently.

They will refer to those who are not tanned as pasty. I wonder if that pastyness has ever stifled a potential job opportunity or relationship. Colorism is a form of prejudice and a cause of discrimination. It causes more division in a world that is divided enough. Some say colorism has its roots in colonialism. Others say colorism still disrupts unity and opportunity in the black community. I feel as though black people use colorism more than white people when communicating amongst ourselves. Others just use racism as a catch all crowd control.

PANDORA'S PURPOSE

Is it ok for men to express emotions like fear and regret?

Better yet is it ok to emote love and respect?

In our society we as men are raised to be strong yet blank.

Unpredictable yet reliable, silent but desirable.

Viable while still carrying a note of mystery.

An impossible feet but one that is required to meet society's inquiry.

But what about Pandora's box?

Once unlocked, her contents have been known to rock the very

foundation society stands on.

Sometimes with a bomb but also by the tip of the tongue or a pen.

Man must appear one way to society but another domestically.

Its perplexing G.

You see it is necessary to express what we hold to chest cause if we don't,

society must cash the check in exchange for the contents of Pandora's

box.

I believe our women hold the key. And the lock. And the box.

We just fill her box with the contents of our hearts with the hope she will

guarantee our safekeeping.

By doing this society will never see us weeping.

We can keep our enemy at bay, even if only for one day.

RAW

If I went and purchased a Burberry Modern fit suit and coupled it with Benson Wholecut Oxfords in Black, I would look rather nice; better still I could add a simple platinum jewelry set to set it off. Although this outfit would be very fine how long would the outfit stay in tact in the middle of the Amazon jungle. I am not making an argument against the refined, but out to better understand the balance between raw and refined emotions. Once one removes all material one is left with only the person. To be raw means to be pure.

One can be raw on a physical, mental, and spiritual scale. Concerning physical attributes to be raw means to be pure of body. One should strive to fuel the body with that which is necessary for the body to function. Necessarily this means abstaining from unnecessary chemicals within the body. Regarding the mind one should aim for mental balance through meditation and personal awareness.

Negative thoughts can disrupt a harmonious mental status thus creating thoughts which are not relevant in that person's life in actuality. One must also be in tune with a God source when considering spirituality. If one has no understanding of their spiritual source once the world drains them, they have no power source for them to recharge with. There is nothing wrong with living a refined life, but one must be aware of the impurities within oneself and in their environment. By doing this one can burn away the negative and reinforce the positive.

Look Before You Listen?

When a leader is new to his environment, or when a new individual joins a leader's environment how should the leader go about acquiring information that maintains balance in his system. I have been known to say "Look before you listen; listen before you speak- in that order." Mouths lie, but so do eyes so leaders must be able to communicate objectives and see the results. Do we observe a person before we weigh their opinion? When I meet a person, I want to do business with I must hear what they are talking about, but I must also observe their actions to see if their movement and activities match up with their sensibilities.

That being said should I initially observe the person in action and then allow for conversation or execute the opposite? It should be noted that I will always give clear explanations for what my expectations are- I definitely appreciate follow up questions. At first glance, I would wager that I should observe the person in action to better understand their process before engaging the individual in direct information retrieval. Observing also includes noticing body language and eye contact while I describe the objectives that we need accomplished.

On the other hand, I can open the lines of communication with the individual and allow for an explanation of motives before observing their actions. In this option I express the objectives, listen to their response, engage in dialogue, and then watch their actions to see if their actions run in line with the objectives at hand. Remember, I am considering this question from a leadership position in which the leader is new in his or her environment, or if a new individual is being introduced into the environment. I feel as though wisdom and trust are powerful variables in the communication equation.

Can I apply the same communication equation to a leader in a toxic environment to a situation where the leader's environment is not toxic, but the leader needs information from different angles? I would say absolutely not. Communication is very organic, but at the same time leaders need to establish consistency across the board. Leaders need to know and understand their teammates in order to establish delegation and promotional opportunities. After contemplation I now wager that you should speak into existence; listen at all times, and observe as you speak-this is live action leadership.

This communication equation can be applied during any conversation and can be expressed over time. In a snapshot moment this equation can provide a leader with real time knowledge about the individuals in his environment that is applicable to the objectives at hand. Over time this knowledge can be applied to further delegation and promotion opportunities adding value to the organization. Leaders must use a shrewd eye when considering the value individuals add to their organization as well as the individual's strengths and weaknesses. Live action leadership promotes communication and participation between the team and it's leader. If you look before you listen and listen before you speak you run the risk of prejudging the activity before you witness the outcome. If you speak without listening the conversation may become one-sided and valuable information can be lost.

Active listening is critical. Listening doesn't always mean believing. Sometimes what you see promotes the wrong motive. The wisest leaders know how to seamlessly observe and communicate with team members to achieve objectives adding value to everyone associated with the organization. I believe that the listening equation also includes considerations toward the environment the leader finds himself in. Furthermore, I believe the equation also responds to time. Initially it may behoove the leader to give credibility to team members while deploying observational techniques like those spoken about above. Over time one can increase or decrease trust and communication as needed with any given individual. Of course, it is impossible to boil communication and team dynamic down to an absolute formula, but it is absolutely interesting to see the balances that can be made and the losses that can be avoided if you assess the notion of what happens when a leader says "Look before you listen; listen before you speak-this in that order."

APORIA'S FRUIT

I met a lady named Aporia, but I am unaffected by her presence in my life.

Her strife caused distrust among men lusting after her understanding.

I over stood their ignorance of her presence and I witnessed her sadist tutelage of hatred.

Accosted by Aporia, doubt spreads fear and distrust like cancer's disgusted seed in Aporia's garden.

The fruits produced stand as abomination to God's plan for Man.

It's byproduct only fit for a madman living on barren land; Aporia's grip is deadly.

She steadily sows the seeds of fear, ignorance, confusion and disconnectedness to steal your benefits and steadfastness.

Judo chop her Kung Fu grip to release yourself from her soul snatching ambassadorship.

Aporia's fruit is only eaten by the weak mind and planted by dictatorship.

ON AMERICAN NATIONALISM

If I held a Nationalism Conference and invited a representative from every Nationalist collective what do you assume would happen? I would have a member of the Black Panther Party sitting next to an Alt-Right supporter across from a Shiite Muslim and a Jew. How much should I spend on security? Before we can consider the value of Nationalism as a construct, we must first understand the concept of Nationalism. There have been many people who have bought in to the concept of Nationalism lately, but may not fully be aware of what it truly means. Furthermore, Nationalist supporters may be unaware of what the social construct is fully capable of producing if left misunderstood and to its own devices.

Nationalism can be defined as a "loyalty and devotion to a nation especially : a sense of national consciousness exalting one nation above all others and placing primary emphasis on promotion of its culture and interests as opposed to those of other nations". In this definition it can be said that individuals who promote nationalism look to their nation as supreme. Under such a notion one may look at other nation populations as inferior to their own. We live in a fluid multilateral world; such thinking is dangerous. Later the definition says that such intense beliefs can lead to war.

It is also worth noting that a nation can be identified as a group of people who share a common belief structure or land mass. Israel can be considered a nation; a nation can be seen in Palestine. A nation can be a collection of Nations like the USSR. A nation can also be a collection of federations like the United States. Look at the history of Palestine and the Israeli people. Intense Nationalism causes confusion, death and destruction.

Consider this list of notable notorious nationalists from history: Adolf Hitler, Benito Mussolini, Giuseppe Garibaldi, Camillo Benso, count di Cavour, Yasser Arafat, Sun Yat-sen, Giuseppe Mazzini, Gabriel Dumont, Lajos Kossuth, and Charles Stewart Parnell.

Each of these individuals possess a passion- real or falsified- for their respective Nations. Each of them committed atrocities upon others for the sake of their "nation". Adolf Hitler forged a nation that aimed to remove anyone contrary to the master Aryan race. In America right wing Nationalists look to erase any notion of supremacy not connected to the Aryan Race. Donald Trump would like to add his name into the ring as the next installment of Nationalism in a time where other nationalist collectives are rising. But is this a wise political action?

Nationalism calls for an adherence to a set of shared cultural beliefs. Nationalism is translated from generation to generation via parents and social norms. Social norms mirror what popular culture deems appropriate. Therefore, in order to understand the brand of Nationalism someone follows you must look at their history and their current social activities.

We have seen Donald Trump's regard for women in the comments he says about their genitalia as well as the respect level he has for his wife. We know what he has said about minorities at home and abroad. We know his opinion on the majority of working-class Americans. We have witnessed the types of people he chooses to surround himself with as well as what he does with people who disagree with him. His version of Nationalism falls in line with toxic Alt-Right, neo Nazis philosophies. These antiquated beliefs were the cause of WW2. These beliefs opened the door to eugenics. Nationalism can choke international commerce because of its separatist virtue. As stated above we live in a fluid multilateral world. Nationalism was a powerful force contributing to WW2.

Why would our world leaders turn back to a philosophy that tore the world apart once? I am very much proud to be an American. I believe that American is one of the greatest countries on Earth. But I will forever leave room for others to grow. America can still be great while helping others to actualize their greatness. I understand that such a notion is becoming antiquated without national support. We can no longer afford to be Earth's sole police force; it is an unfair request. I propose that we still stand with American pride towards growth. I say we take a step back from international engagement and work on national development. I request that we work with our international policy makers and NGOs to maintain international peace. The international community should be mature enough not to employ the philosophy of "If your not first you're last."

RACISM

If you have long hair I am better than you... How legitimate is this claim? I don't believe that having more hair makes me better than another person. If I cut my fingertip I bleed red; If I cut a white person's fingertip he will bleed red as well. We have identical biological makeup. We have a similar psychological composure as well. We both need food, water, and oxygen to survive. People tend to thrive in communities although communal living is not necessary for an adult human being's survival. This being said it is illogical for racism to exist.

Google states racism is defined as prejudice, discrimination, or antagonism directed against someone of a different race based on the belief that one's own race is superior. To presuppose superiority to another solely on race is ignorance. It is safe to say that all people are different from one another, also to include skin tones. It is not apparent nor valid to say that one group of people is superior to another solely because of their skin color, religious affiliation, or sexual preference. The fruit of such philosophy is ignorance and hatred. Such emotions shouldn't be passed to our youth. Such ideas will not promote true competition and societal improvement. I am an American African and I live in Atlanta. My neighbor may be an American Caucasian.

We may be different from one another in skin tone, but we are similar in many other features. Furthermore, if our neighborhood were to be invaded by Russian supporters from South and Central America would color differences matter more than our American similarities? I believe if were were invaded most Americans would come together to destroy the threat to our sovereignty. If we would come together to destroy such a threat what stops us today? Does it take America crumbling for us to become whole?

BEAUTIFUL SUFFERING

Isn't it interesting how well God knows his creation? I have led a very colorful life thus far. God has positioned every challenge and its success so perfectly that the conclusions I now reach are outlandish yet attainable. I faced challenges in my childhood who's lessons are still applicable till today. I did battle with challenges in my young adult life that either reinforced my childhood victories or brought new understanding to an old question. My only problem is God's communication style... The more the problem burdens me the brighter the solution shines, but nothing is spoken straight forward.

For me, God's instructions and purpose for my life is now hammering at the front door of my mind with a sledgehammer. It's not always so simple. His instruction for self improvement and empowerment is usually connected to a vice that is causing a disturbance in our lives. God puts us through experiences to show us we are strong enough to weather them. After that, God puts those who weather the test in the lives of others as support. God needs people who are not ashamed to speak on the true nature of their circumstances, even if they have not made it through the storm yet. People can find strength in the faithfulness of others, especially when those who are favored- they are aware of where their favor comes from and they know where to issue their blessings to reinforce the faithfulness of others engaged in the struggle.

NEW YEAR'S PLAN

Last year was above average as it was a bit Savage but I was ravaged by the blessings of the Most High.

Many times I questioned why I had to be tested by fire about my earthly desires and tried by heat if I could share my few good graces with the masses.

My mind bridges through time to the man who gave his lunch so Jesus could feed the many for i'll bet he had an interesting upcoming year.

It's a new year, but I am the same man and I stand to keep the same plan from the year before- I hope to expand my understanding.

Man love's to have absolute plans but that hand belongs to God; man should plan for the unknown with an open mind and a loving heart.

Last year I learned to have faith in God's hands while holding on to becoming a better man... I let go of full control, but held on to the Serenity Prayer.

I understand that this year God will present me with opportunities and obstacles that will further mold me into the man I am supposed to be, not the man I intend to see.

I greet the challenge with open hands because in letting go of full control I am better able to express the blessings of God's infinite love that choked me in the past.

I cast my worries from the past into God's hands opening my own hands up for the blessings from above.

I raise my head to witness my guardian angel, holy messenger to my father up above guaranteeing me safe travels through the year.

I clear my mind and follow the instruction given to me with an open mind, a loving heart, and receiving hands for this immaculate year.

Amen.

I GET IT

Why would a God of infinite power and wisdom create an object with the sole purpose of praising him?

Why would an everlasting word be spoken into existence for the benefit of objects blessed with free will?

I get it.

Like a best friend who provides everything for another only wishing to be thanked in return.

I get it.

For all the blessings he has been given and for the many sins he's been forgiven, through Him we are forgiven but we have forgotten.

I get it.

We wallow in self-pity and we draw out our suffering as if it is our own cross to bear.

We were meant to share it, but we forgot where we come from; our inheritance lost to our ignorance through the ages.

I get it.

Like a mother who bears a child, or or the father who rears the child all they ask in return is remembrance and gratefulness.

I get it.

We forget where we come from, drumming up hell where heaven and favor could be.

I get it.

I thank him every day. It is free and fulfilling.

Thank him.

I remember the struggle laced in favor.

Through the struggle there are lessons for heaven and blessings

unlimited.

I love it.

Focus the energy in your mind.

Ten count breath in ten count breath out.

Blackout the voices in your head.

They forever shout out code red.

You move faster until your mind and hands bled.

Find center and enter serenity.

Peace is enemy to the evils of this world.

Breath.

Let the troubles and pressures of this world melt away.

Find that moment of clarity in the sea of disarray.

Trade in the voices of many and tune into the one true voice.

Rejoice knowing we all share a psychic connection between ourselves and our creator.

The farther away from the source the weaker the connection.

Consider the attraction of magnets; the closer they are to each of the stronger the force.

If you put twelve magnets in a bag and got a bigger magnet over the group what happens?

My admonition notes the minor magnets react to one another while still responding to major force.

Of course I believe the same psychic correlation exists between God and Man.

You must come to over stand you are not the soul force in God's master

plan.

Ban the voices of the many.

Breath in ten count, breath out ten count.

Steady your mind, Steady your hand.

You may paint stick figures by your hand or tap into the psychic source

and reveal a portion of God's master plan.

Can you stand to be still?

LIFE AND DEATH

Life is more like a beautiful tragedy ending in death. They are two ends of the same dilemma. In it's creation absolutely nothing is certain. Death is an absolute certainty. As we move through life some possibilities open up while others close shut. Life's journeyers have no full control of their dilemma, but death's persistent presence stifles us the closer we get to is finality.

BLESSINGS

I was having breakfast at a pancake house one morning. Granted my morning did not start off on great footing but I was ready to attack my day with zest. I love people watching so I couldn't help but notice the demographic breakdown of pancake house I was in: approximately three quarters Caucasian while the other was an assortment of Moorish, Latino, and Asian. I was the only black male, and I always feel as though the reputation of the black male was on the line with every gesture I made.

One table had two white guys in their fifties or early sixties while another had two Latino ladies. Two tables were white couples. I spoke quietly to mask my dominance. I ordered my breakfast from the Moorish server and proceeded to delve into my social media. While I was eating and tweeting a lady at one of the white couple tables sneezed. Quietly I said "God bless you". She said thank you and we both proceeded with our meals. I found it interesting how no one else spoke up, but I left it at that. The server waited till I was finished and asked if I was ready for the check. She brought the check and I gave up my debit card. Again, I waited on my card but it seemed to be taking longer than usual. When the server returned, she gave my card and my receipt with a note on it which read " Thanks for your blessings." I smiled and left the pancake house.

The situation got me to thinking. What was it that inclined the lady to do this? I didn't think it was my race or my age. I didn't think it was out of spite or out of malice. I feel as though her gesture was one of gratitude for God's blessing, and the need to share that blessing with others. I feel as though my behavior expressed quality home training and dignity- two qualities that can be wanting in today's society. Always remember that you have been blessed by others. Always remember that you have had high points and low points. There have been times when you needed an extra push. There have been times when you could give an extra push. These are the reasons God blesses those who bless others; some call this karma. It is imperative that we bless each other. By doing this our community would be more stable; children will view this behavior as normal and required.

People are conduits for psychic power.

Are we not certain as to which points of the body that can deliver soul power?

With a mental alter one can achieve mental clarity.

It is imperative to control your psychic weaponry.

Certainly once the mind is at rest and there is serenity you may caress and test what parts of the body fill out of whack or supercharged.

You can harbor minerals, spices and herbs. Yes, you can introduce oil and or water to find the proper mixture.

No mineral, spice, or herb stands as a fixture in the energy point awakening.

Old wise men painstakingly composed knowledge connecting body to body, body to soul, soul to soul, and soul to source

Understanding the source of psychic connection is detrimental in understanding original godlike mightiness.

I attest laying hands to to head neck and chest offsets psychic fire.

Then transpire said fire throughout the body.

Awaken the soul through bold strokes.

Sometimes sensual pain stirs the psyche.

WHEN THE DEVIL PLAYED A GAME WITH GOD AND MAN

And Satan said on to God "Let us play a game of tug of war, but with a twist."

Understanding the duelist, God said "But of course. What are the terms and conditions?"

Satan responds "My admonition is the power of free souls. Original clean souls burn the brightest."

Delighted God responds "Clean souls are also the hardest to control, are you bold enough to wrestle them from the body and myself?"

Satan jeers "You gave them so much wealth, and us so little. What favor will grant me to even the scales?"

God curtails "Some souls regard us as fairytales so you, Satan will stand at one end and I on the other. Man will stand in the middle tugging towards his desire."

Satan fires "Where is the sport in all that?"

God answers back " You will tug with all your might at their souls, but I will use my pinky to draw them closer to me. We will see where they land when their bodies surrender free will."

Satan beggs "Which soul is the number one contender, pretender of the good life?"

God delights "You see my friend over there? He is the one most similar to my Son- blessed and highly favored. Try to taper him; draw your rope."

Satan Snickers "I hope your faith is as strong as his conviction; my vipers are already on him. Their souls are as dark as night, therefore they do not burn; they only smolder."

Colder the man cried out "Why do they hate me? I see the end of my suffering similar to Sisyphus, but people keep kicking the boulder back. Who should I contact before my back cracks?"

Satan Attacks the rope "This is not a Goddamn joke God I will drag him, jack him, and molest his family members!"

God was silent, but drew is pinky closer to his heart.

"Who fights for me? I can barely push a pound and yet this boulder weighs a ton. I sweat but I can not run. God give me strength." He lit a blunt.

Satan cheered "Look at him. He runs to drugs and not you. Bid his soul adieu."

God smiles knowing ignorance and arrogance are two of Satan's favorite traits. "Wait."

"I smoke to blunt the pain of the world, it is too much to carry. I can not terry like the mighty Atlas. I may shrug and let my people down."

God smiled and tugged harder. The man would never forsake God nor his people. The man just did not feel equal.

Deceitfully Satan whispered "God does not love you equally, give in peacefully to the world and it is yours."

The man yelled back "this is not your world to give, but it is ours to suffer in"

Satan snapped at the rope "Shut your mouth and surrender. Your faith is tied to a pretender. My storm you can not take flight from. Bondage is all you know. Accept this." He hissed.

God leaned down and kissed the man's forehead as it bled. "Take comfort and draw your sword." God tugged harder, but only because the man tugged harder. With the rope fully tightened the man drew his God Sword given to him at birth and sliced what he thought was a boulder. It was a rope- a chain. And it was broken.

Satan shrieked "You cheated God! You gave him a sword to cut my chain!"

God laughed "You named the game and I named the conditions. The sword was given to him at birth."

They thought I was defeated for in my time off loss I became numb to this Earth- I went in search of rebirth.

In solidarity I went to my quiet place to vent to God and find myself. I felt dangerous, fully charged but lacking life's direction.

Making connections I recognize life's a Pendulum, and to every loss there are forever wins.

Seeing that God's blessings are truly heaven sent fragment hate from heart for we are here today, yet gone tomorrow.

Abandon hate from heart knowing God's love commands letting go of sorrow. Make room with wisdom and knowledge for grace and compassion; sow love into Earth and just watch what grows.

Will you speak the words of God or continue to watch the world burn for I have learned that faith lacking action causes major distractions in our hearts.

Follow the commandments of love and they make hearts sing. I scream the blessings of the Lord in my life and yours, absorb God's power in your life and the spirit will guide you right.

As a spiritual knight I will never fully understand God's light but I accept his master plan. God sends Angels to Earth to shed love over his people.

Holy love has no equal so I connect to it knowing the feeling is heaven sent. Praise God that I went and vent to him, because I made space for heavenly love to swim through me. Now I pour heavenly energy into the seeds of love that we sowed let us see what we grow.

ON CONVERSATION AND RELIGION

I often take Lyft as a supplement to public transit. More often than not I pose questions to the driver or the group at large just to sample public opinion. In my last encounter I had the opportunity to ride with an African American male aged around 23 to 30. He mentioned that he was Muslim so I took an interest in expanding on the conversation. I was only able to get two or three questions deep before he flung his defensive wall up.

The driver says "I don't mean to be rude, but could we not talk about religion? It makes me uncomfortable." Out of ten improv conversations two or three conversations would end in this fashion. The conversation ended so abruptly that awkward silence filled the rest of the ride; the driver got one star, but that's beyond the point. Earlier in the week I had a similar conversation with a lady but we shared an open dialogue that taught me a much more about Islam.

I'm Christian yet I wrestled with expressing curiosity about other religions. We as a nation gain cultural solidarity from engaging in open dialogue about our cultural differences. We do not have to have the same beliefs to have civil conversations. Granted the Lyft driver may not have been in a conversational mood at the time, or it could have been my approach. I just found his disposition interesting and I wanted to know his rationale as to how he got to his spiritual conclusion.

Can It be said that religion and social norms go hand in hand? I understand that I only know one religion intimately, and am well acquainted with a couple of others. I believe that individuals should be allowed to believe whatever they like so long as their belief structure doesn't conflict with my daily live; they can pray to whoever they like so long as our social norms are left in tact. In the Christian community we are taught to love our brothers and sisters as we love ourselves. We are instructed to do this in order to achieve a more Godlike community.

If we as Christians believed in this one particular law our society would flow more consistently. In American society we believe that there is a separation between the church and the state. As such we cannot directly inject the 10 Commandments into legislation passable by the Senate, but we can look at the values in religion and assume proper living guidelines for the general public. Consider Judaism and Islam. It is not passable in any of those beliefs for a man to steal another man's wife without proper redress.

Furthermore, it is unethical to kill another man without proper reasoning least you suffer the consequences. If you look at a variety of religious doctrines you will note that many of their social values match, but their deities and stories differ. We don't even have to exclude doctrines that don't branch from the Judeo-Christian tree. You can find quality social norms in Hinduism and Confucianism as well. There are some negative religious doctrines in each religion, but mankind has negative tendencies. We look to religion as a reference to the good life, but we can't agree on the story. More so you don't have to believe in a religion to know how to construct positive social responsibility. We have a responsibility to keep the fabric of society in tact, but we use religion as a division instead of glue.

CONSIDERING CREATIVITY

People say "Do what you love, and you'll never work a day in your life." Do you know the amount of faith and intelligence required to follow a dream through a toxic environment? In today's world people are challenged with providing for their immediate needs while putting away for their future needs in an economy in attraphy- usually at the detriment of their personal dreams or artistic expressions. It is almost as though people who choose to create are rarely blessed with the commodity of time.

Those who do not have such a luxury have to sacrifice: sleep, fun, food, luxury, and the like. That or have luck on their side. I have heard "Luck favors the well prepared". I wholeheartedly agree with this statement. If you are in such a creative predicament hustle and support are critical. Being in a toxic environment can either hinder or refine creativity. If I have knowledge, a network of individuals, and ambition at my disposal I should be well prepared to create should the required resources present themselves. As is the nature of art; it must be expressed with deliberate passion. This is to say that we should encourage the expression of art whenever possible and have the courage to share our own expressions with others. By doing this more people will get the opportunity to do what inspires them more regularly. Discovering the voice of your expression is a beautiful story.

DESERT FLOWERS

In the dryest of locations beauty still resides in the eye of the creator.
In the amphitheatre of the harshest environments God embraced the
Earth and sowed seeds of beautiful life that could withstand time's
brutality connected to the after life.
Beautiful wildlife brought to life with the Earth as the midwife; God the
Father as the pallbearer shedding tears of joy for her midterm.
Life is a beautiful moment so grasp it, life's so short it's tragic, but at the
right moment it's magic.
Attraction to God is magnetic for he created us in his image blessing
desert flowers with beautiful coats protecting us from the desert storm.
Heaven adorned the Earth with sweet the nectar of hope.
Blessed with love good enough for the demigods angels were confused as
the Titans were as to why God would create a spirit forever connected to
the after life.
They shed tears of pain counted as rain sustaining life and preserving
beauty.
It is their duty to love us though we are all unaware of the blessing God
gave us; know for certain that this life has it's curtains.
As we die we return to Earth's dirt though it may seem cursed to go back
to dirt for we to must feed Terra Firma to bring new spirit to retake Earth
as wife as we walk with God in his beautiful after life.

SOUL SURGEON

The body is an incredible machine so what does that mean to the soul?

The loophole ties the to together, separate but when brought together made whole.

Who do we console when the body is sick, weak, or accosted?

We see the doctor to receive diagnosis and proper redress.

They run tests to assess the situation, and after contemplation they suggest a surgeon.

Using the burden of truth the surgeon sees objectively.

To the situation at hand with the proper plan to save the body.

But to separate body from soul is to disembody the whole.

So who do you see when the soul goes cold to bring negative and positive charge to the soul's psyche.

I wager one must go to a pastor and from a pastor to a Woli because he connects to the soul and body having answered the call and gained knowledge.

Protege to the game.

Graduated from the school of hard knocks.

Sent by God to repair the soul and keep the Constitution whole.

Bold surgeon removes or implants to keep whole.

Woli connects to body and soul with the same goal.

He atolls the sickness unto death in attempts to bring peace to the soul.

Not only is Woli surgeon, but also soldier.

Administrator to God's order to guarantee peace and prosperity by any means necessary.

Very deadly to the enemy of peace.

He forever tarries through the world's trouble.

Humbly he goes to God to recharge; aggressively he releases light to darkness.

With ever loving arms he touches people.

Remember that Woli has been stress tested by the Devil and God.

Now and forever there is no equal to God's charge, Woli is blessed teacher, surgeon and soldier. Praise God.

HEAVENLY ENERGY

Heavenly Energy has entered me.

Heavenly Father, all blessed be.

To be redeemed and hear heaven speak but to be so cursed to see angels weep.

All of heaven's tears wash over me, peacefully all my fears begin leave.

Faithfully everloving hope flows from me to you.

Can't you connect to me through our shared Heavenly Energy entity.

Interestingly God's energy entered me.

Complete the circle with me to you through speaking heavenly love from up above.

God's love is eternal, let heavenly energy enter your soul. It will reverb throughout your body probably frightening at first. The power of the Lord is a blessing to the soul. It's open to us all but we must all stand tall and love one another.

Like a brother from another mother we must profess love for each other and bless one another while abandoning begrudging hate towards each other.

Society's seems to be bursting at its seams but heavenly love stands as the seamstress that can repair the very fabric of our souls making us whole but better than ever before.

Devilish hate destroys us all like a category four hurricane, stand tall in the blessings of the the Lord because his hope will repel the the very power of the storm and repair all of the damages done.

With the force of C4 I explode love over hate, set a date with my maker to recover the heavenly energy with my father for holy love is rechargeable.

Unanalyzable to the human eye I reflect on the true depth of holy love; unclassifiable to the human mind holy love forever stands against the grain of father time.

Take pride knowing this love is sent to us on heavenly wings from above.

It's meant for us to tap into, it's heavenly message sent to our mental eye.

Heavenly love is meant to be spoken over each other all the fucking time.

Tears fill my eyes as heavenly love burns it's image in my heart pumping power in my veins encouraging me to remain in the same lane of God's intelligent design.

BLESSINGS BROUGHT TO LIGHT

The sun was shining when I woke up but it was dark when I closed my eyes.

In darkness and cold I stayed bold during the struggle.

Trouble bubbled up through the darkness but I understood steadfastness.

I knew that with God I would get past the iniquities; the sun would soon shine.

Unreliable haters call my line telling me Father Time was dying.

They're lying trying to get me to forget the ever brightening grace of God and light.

Fright never crossed my eyes because I was wise enough to understand time.

Forever sublime I created in the darkness and stopped to rest my mind.

I arise to a new day, a new play to make born of dusk light.

The sunlight made new birth shine ever brighter, praise God I am a fighter.

Often times I would create with little more sight produced from that of a lighter.

With backbiters ever present through the darkness in light their souls appeared starving like peasants.

The light feeds me like a king. I absorb as much hope as I can as I stand in God's grace.

I stay ready, charged up for darker days.

Adeshina's Admonition

Beware the consequences of cutthroat capitalism and compassion's absence. Such casualties leave scars in flesh and atrophy in economys. Mankind is always at its strongest when we embrace love and wisdom within society. Interestingly it is only through pain and suffering that mankind's true nature comes to light- good or bad. I have seen both sides of the coin; I hope I have given light to both and a charge to challenge normality in our increasingly changing society. Thank you, and good day.

In Blood,
Adeshina I. M. Lawal

Made in the USA
Middletown, DE
07 April 2021